The Simple Guide to Visual Journaling

(even if you aren't an artist)

Cathy Hutchison

Printed in the United States of America

First Printing, 2018

ISBN: 1546965254
ISBN-13: 978-1546965251

alacris

alacrispublishing.com

Dedication

For Michael Lagocki,
who inspired me to start carrying a box of crayons
and continues to save the world through comics.

I'm so glad you picked up this book...

When I first started journaling visually, I couldn't draw anything. ***Seriously.***

But it didn't matter. After all, I was just creating notes for myself.

The thing is, suddenly, every meeting became more engaging.

I was more focused, had better recall, and as I started to experiment, using my notebook for more than just meeting notes, I discovered the incredible power of thinking on paper.

My friend, you don't have to be an artist to journal visually.

No one has to label you "creative" or give you an "A" in art class.

All you need is a little bit of instruction.

This book is designed to get you from zero to visually journaling on your own...fast!

Enjoy,
Cathy Hutchison

Contents

What makes visual journaling so powerful? 1

Tools to get started 7

Working with the words 11

Enhance pages with embellishment 17

Rediscover your visual vocabulary 23

Create symbols for people 29

Simple layout techniques 35

Different ways to journal 41

Journaling exercises to get you started 47

The benefits of visual journaling 59

Ideas for pictograms and ideograms 61

Chapter 1

What makes visual journaling so powerful?

Visual journaling takes us off of auto-pilot.

We live much of our lives on auto-pilot—which for some things is effective. After all, if we had to wake up every morning and really think about removing the toothpaste cap, putting the paste on our brush, scrubbing each molar, and rinsing our mouth out, we would never get anywhere on time.

Automating processes is something that our brains do very well.

It saves time, and frees up our mental resources for other things.

However, we can wind up living too much of our lives on auto-pilot.

When that happens our days blur together. We move from task to task to task—feeling like a hamster in a wheel—as our lives become one long run-on sentence without the periods and pauses that help us comprehend the meaning.

The most authentic part of us—the part that dreams, enjoys and feels gratitude—can get lost as we go through the motions.

Visual journaling reconnects us with ourselves.

It focuses our intention on our thoughts, feelings, and actions.

It shines a spotlight on our current path.

It helps us take stock of our experiences, the information we've consumed, and the tasks we perform daily so that we get the macro view of where things are going—giving us the opportunity to course-correct if we don't like our trajectory.

Why explore visual journaling instead of simply writing words?

While journaling with words has power, there are reasons that visual journaling is more powerful.

We are biologically wired to be visual.

More than 50 percent of the cortex—the surface of the brain—is devoted to processing visual information, which shouldn't be surprising. We experience this every day.

There is a Chinese proverb that says: *What I hear, I forget. What I see, I remember. What I do, I understand.* Add visuals to your journal, and you are much more likely to remember the content.

Visuals can reveal the underlying structure better than words.

Have you ever tried mind-mapping? It's a technique for brainstorming ideas (usually with software or sticky notes), then organizing the ideas by linking similar thoughts together. Mind-mapping is a popular technique because it reveals the underlying structure of ideas in a way that lines of text or spoken words cannot.

My friend, Michael Lagocki, is a graphic facilitator. He has scribed for Fortune 500 corporations and some of the most popular authors in the country. (He's not just *a* scribe. He is **the** scribe.)

Michael shares the story of scribing a merger negotiation where the two sides were experiencing a disconnect. Michael handed a marker to the president of

Company A and asked him to draw how he saw the merger.

The president of Company A took the marker and drew this:

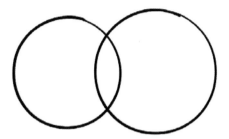

Michael then handed the marker to the president of Company B with the same request, who drew this:

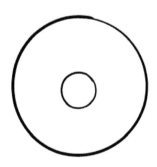

Suddenly, everyone in the room could see why the parties weren't able to agree: they were talking about completely different structures. And that knowledge radically improved the conversation. Both sides redirected toward determining a structure that both could live with.

Visual journaling can have the same effect. As you "think" on paper, you will see things you may not have seen before.

Drawing creates a "state" change.

Drawing shifts us from the left brain (the side of the brain that governs analytical thought and language) to the right brain (the side of the brain in charge of perception and meaning).

When we write in our journals, we begin with the left brain in our thinking, but the moment we leave language and enter the world of symbols and embellishment, we engage the right side. "Whole brain" thinking (using *both* sides of our brains) creates richer context .

In a digital world, we appreciate the simplicity and tactile experience of creating by hand.

There is something to the kinesthetic act of touching paper. There is a physical experience when we write or draw by hand that more deeply connects us to the content.

Does it seem curious to you that the more digital our world has become, the more popular analog planners and physical journals have become?

Don't get me wrong—I love my screens. But I've found that the more reliant I've become on my digital assistants and all of the magical things they do, the more I've enjoyed the physical simplicity of crayons and paper.

What most people mean when they say they "can't draw" is that they aren't able to duplicate a sketch they've seen or recreate their favorite superhero on paper.

Unless we were labeled "artist" early on, most of us stopped drawing after the first time we tried to create something in school and produced results that weren't what we hoped they would be.

We looked over at someone else's paper and decided they had artistic talent and we didn't. Then, we opted out.

Guess what?

Part of the magic of visual journaling is that your skill level doesn't matter.

Right this minute, give yourself permission to be a terrible artist.

Absolutely, stinking terrible.

Truly dreadful.

So bad that if someone sees your work, you will have to burn it.

a message for everyone who "can't draw"

Can you write the letter M? What about Q? If so, you can draw.

Whenever I teach workshops on visual journaling, people always apologize for their lack of ability.

Take the pressure off. Your journal is for you. Imperfection is actually desirable.

Just as you wouldn't expect your grocery list to be published and hit the New York Times® Best Seller list, don't expect your art to be ready for mass-market either.

The visual elements in your journal don't need to become world-famous pieces of art. They are meant to help you process your thoughts and to more effectively engage with whatever you are journaling.

Here's a bit of good news:

It will only take about 20 hours of visual journaling for you to become competent.

According to Josh Kauffman (author of the *The First 20 Hours*, 2013):

"You can go from knowing absolutely nothing to performing noticeably well in a very short period of time: approximately 20 hours, often less."

That's good news for those of us who "can't draw."

And—want to know a secret?

I am part of that tribe.

Just doing it without caring about what it looked like is how I went from terrible to competent.

Want a peek inside my first notebooks?

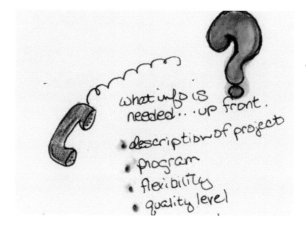

Sample from one of my early attempts at visually journaling meeting notes.

Sample from one of my first scribing efforts with a client. (The ponytail on the programmer still makes me laugh.)

1. Visual journaling takes us off autopilot.

2. Visual journaling helps us notice things about ourselves.

3. We are wired to be visual.

4. Visuals can reveal underlying structure better than words.

5. Drawing creates a state change.

6. a tactile experience has impact in a digital world.

7. a lack of drawing skill doesn't matter a bit.

● ● ●

Chapter 2

Tools to get started

You probably have perfectly functional visual journaling tools lying around your house. (If you have kids, you can raid their stash.)

But there is something a little wonderful about new supplies dedicated to a purpose, so you may want to pick these up through your favorite online retailer or at a local craft or office supply store.

Start with these four tools:

1. A black pen that writes easily

Over the years, I've test-driven many different black pens. You are looking for one that glides across a page and puts down a true black ink.

(Bonus points if it doesn't bleed through the paper.)

My favorites include Faber-Castell's PITT artist pens, Pilot Precise V7 Rolling Ball pens, Paper Mate's InkJoy pens, and the Staedtler Triplus Fineliner.

There's a good chance that you will wind up trying different pens over time until you discover your personal favorite.

2. Colored pencils, markers, or crayons

Next, you need a method of adding color to your journal. This not only gives the pages character and depth, but also improves retention and evokes emotion.

Colored pencils and crayons have the benefit of not bleeding through paper. Prismacolor brand colored pencils are my personal favorite and while more expensive than their school-supply counterparts, they lay down serious color on a page.

If you are a marker fan, just select a journal with thicker paper.

When I first started visual journaling, I threw a box of Crayola crayons in my purse. They were cheap and served the purpose. However, the box got beat up as it traveled with me, and the crayons broke easily—until I discovered that crayons fit neatly in a cigarette case. Then they became my "executive crayons."

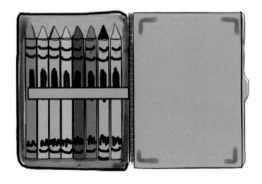

3. A notebook

To start, you can choose the most affordable spiral notebook available to you.

If you decide to upgrade to a high quality brand (like Moleskine, Leuchtturm, Field Notes, Midori, or Strathmore), here are some options to consider:

Size

The size you choose should factor in how much space you enjoy "thinking on" cross referenced with portability.

Popular sizes include 8.5 x 11 inches—the same size you used in school; 5 x 8.25 inches—the size favored by architects; and 3 x 5.5 inches—the size of a passport (so you can carry it in your pocket).

Covers

There is the basic choice between hard or soft cover—which can be a decision between bulk and durability.

However, some notebook brands sell fancy, durable shells that allow you to switch out your softer-cover notebooks as you fill them up.

Paper

Different journal brands have different thicknesses of paper, and some brands offer multiple thicknesses.

You also have options in terms of the marks on the page. Choose between ruled (lines, like the notepaper you used in school), squared (like graph paper), dotted, or plain.

For visual journaling, dotted pages offer a nice subtle grid that doesn't get in the way of your thoughts.

Plain pages create a nice open field for shaping whatever you create.

4. A brush pen (with black or light gray ink)

Brush pens are used in calligraphy. You can also find brush markers in colors other than black. Copic and Tombow are popular brands that are available at a wide array of craft and art stores.

A brush pen gives you the ability to add shadow or draw thick lines—which adds flair to simple drawings , headings and block quotes. A black brush pen can create dimension like the on this arrow:

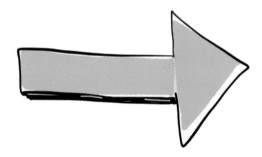

A gray brush pen can be used to draw a shadow beneath the pencil cup to anchor it.

Ready to do this? Let's get started!

☑ Get a black pen that's enjoyable to write with.

☑ Get a notebook that's easy to keep with you all the time.

☑ Get markers, pencils or crayons to add color to your journal.

☐ Optional: Get a black or gray brush marker.

Chapter 3

Working with the words

The majority of your journal is going to be words:

Insights.

Ideas.

Observations.

Goals.

Aspirations.

(Or maybe it will just be your task list, or notes from this morning's meeting.)

The words are the heart of the journal and you will format them much the same way that magazines do. You will create your own personal method for writing body text, headings and subheadings.

First, create your personal body text style.

We are trained from the time we start reading to recognize "body text." It's where the bulk of the content lives. Headings and subheadings break it up to help make sense of the page, but the core content is in lines of black text.

So, let's develop yours.

In the following exercises, you will begin to create a visual style sheet for yourself.

Exercise: What's your 10pt Arial?

Most word-processing programs have a "normal" font style used for body text. (In fact, you are reading my normal font now.)

Pull out a piece of paper that you can recycle later.

Black is the color we are used to identifying with content, so for this exercise, I recommend that you pull out a black pen that writes easily. (Keep in mind, this is your personal journal, if you would prefer purple, roll with it.) The point is to be consistent with what you use for body text in your journaling, to make it easy to visually separate the main content from the navigational elements of the page.

Write the following sentence as fast as you can:

The quick brown dog jumps over the lazy fox.

(Yes, this is a twist the classic keyboarding exercise. I've always felt the dog was unfairly maligned.)

The quick brown dog jumps over the lazy fox.

Look at the sentence. How do you feel about your efforts?

Try it again more slowly.

The quick brown dog jumps over the lazy fox.

Did your results improve or is it the same?

Now write this sentence in a variety of ways. Try:

- All caps.

- Caps and lower case, print.

- The swoopiest cursive you can manage.

- Slanted, as if italic.

- As if a scientist needed the information in this sentence to save the world.

Now, review your results.

- Do you prefer one of the versions?

- Are some easier to read than others?

- Do any feel particularly like you?

Remember, this will take time. The more you journal, the more you will see your personal body text develop. In other words, just practice and it will emerge. No stress involved.

describe what the page or next few pages will be about—and use techniques to make it stand out.

Here are a few ways to make a headline pop:

Make it big.

Next, create your heading styles.

In a magazine layout, a headline (or "heading") provides the overall topic to which the rest of the information on the page relates.

It's a navigation device that allows us to flip through multiple pages and either find an article we are looking for or browse topics to help us identify where we want to stop and read.

Use all caps.

Headings

In a magazine or newspaper, the headline text is usually bigger and bolder than other elements on the page, making it the first thing you see.

In visual journaling, the heading serves the same purpose.

You use a few words (or a single word) to

Put a box around it.

Write it, then drop in a shadow with a colored pencil or marker.

Write it in bubble letters.

Add some stars (or other symbols) to each end of the header.

Underline it.

Subheadings

Like headings, subheadings are major points of information that usually have some smaller text beneath them. You can use the same techniques for subheadings that you use for headings, but on a lesser scale.

It allows you to promote a word or phrase in importance over the general text on the page. This will draw your eye and give a clue as to what is in the block of text that follows.

Exercise: Design a heading style and a subheading style that you can draw quickly.

In your journaling, you will likely play with a variety of heading styles, but for this exercise you will come up with a few heading styles that you can draw quickly.

Pull out a piece of paper that you can recycle later.

With your black pen, write the word HEADING, using some of the variations listed in this part of the chapter.

Are some easier to use than others? Do you have a personal preference? Which ones are the fastest for you to implement?

Play with drop caps.

Have you ever seen an embellished manuscript? The kind with full illustrations and pretty scrolling on the sides? In books like these, the first letter of a chapter often takes up to three lines and is indented into the paragraph.

This is called a drop cap.

Whether your personal style of visual journaling is elegant, folk-art, minimalist, or wildly eccentric, you can come up with a drop cap style that works for you.

Exercise: Create a drop cap.

Get a piece of paper that you will save for reference later.

Index cards work particularly well because they have some weight to them, which makes them easy to draw on.

Draw a capital A about 2 – 3 inches high to give yourself room to work on embellishment.

Now extend the right side of the letter to give it some width.

Give the left leg a step to stand on and color in both the step and the right side of the letter.

Embellish the letter by adding dots and lines.

Use your brush marker to give the letter depth by adding shadow. Imagine a light source to the right top of the letter and put the shadow where you think it would fall if the letter were 3-dimensional.

Here's what a drop cap looks like on a journal page:

This is just one style of drop cap. You could even box it. The options are endless.

Recap

1. Write most of your words in black ink and develop your personal "normal" font.

2. Come up with headings you can create quickly. Here's an at-a-glance cheat sheet:

ALLCAPS

BiG

BOXED

BUBBLE

STARRED

SHADOW

UNDERLINED

BRACKETED

3. Play with drop caps and find a style that suits you: formal, folksy, modern.

Chapter 4

Enhance pages with embellishment

Embellishment is a big part of what makes visual journaling visual.

Bubbles, boxes, horizontal lines, and arrows visually highlight connections. They emphasize some ideas over others and make the information easier to process and remember.

They can also create the navigation system of your notebook.

Using page borders as a notebook navigation system

Let's say that you use your visual journal for EVERYTHING in your life.

You carry one single notebook and record:

- Your daily to-do lists
- Notes from conversations with mentors and friends
- Ideas for your latest project
- Your step count and workouts
- The books you've read
- Podcasts you've listened to

- Inspirational quotes
- Notes from a workshop or class
- Your personal vision board
- Monthly or weekly goals
- Gift ideas for family and friends

For a notebook with a lot of different types of content, embellishments like page borders can help you quickly identify what type of content lives on which page.

There are two orientations for page borders:

Horizontal

Horizontal borders can label a single page, or cover two pages to form a spread. ("Spread" is a magazine term for two pages the reader sees as a single layout.)

Vertical

Vertical page borders are easily seen when you flip through a journal. You can create a system where you use one on every page to indicate content, or only use them on certain pages to make them pop out from the rest.

One technique for creating vertical page borders (if you don't want to draw them) is to use thin, patterned masking tape (also called washi tape).

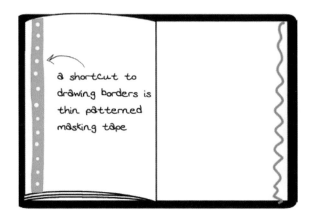

a shortcut to drawing borders is thin patterned masking tape

Use boxes, brackets, clouds and bubbles to make information pop.

Journaling isn't the same as writing an article. It is a thought capture. So, usually there are many different random thoughts on a page.

Boxes, brackets, clouds, and bubbles can be used to separate a single thought on a page, or make it pop visually.

While you will play with your own methods of calling out information, here are a few basic ideas:

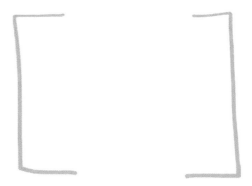

Brackets work well when you are moving quickly or don't have a lot of space. (Or if you are just tired of circles and bubbles.)

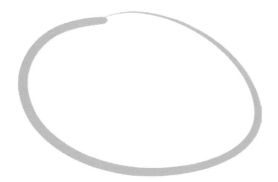

Circles are one of the first methods we learn to use to highlight information. (You probably had *many* worksheets in elementary school where you had to, for example, find an adverb and circle it.)

Boxes have no wasted space. You can fit words all the way to the edges. If you want to uplevel a box, you can embellish it easily.

Bubbles are the circle's fancier cousin. They are useful to indicate thought or to highlight incomplete ideas.

Use horizontal lines to begin a new layout on a partially filled page.

Horizontal lines are an easy way to reclaim wasted space.

You can style them however you like:

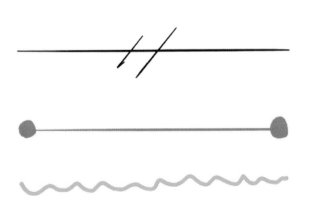

Use arrows to connect ideas.

There are a number of ways to draw arrows.

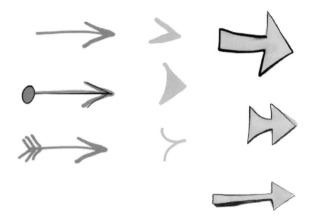

Arrows are effective for connecting separate but related thoughts, showing thoughts which continue on the next page, or pointing attention to a piece of information.

Exercise: Create a page with six of your favorite quotes and use the techniques in this chapter to make each quote pop.

Grab an 8.5 x 11 piece of paper. Ideally, it is unlined, but whatever you have handy will do.

Fold the paper in half vertically, then flatten it straight again. The fold will have created a subtle line directly down the center of the page which you will use as a guide for your columns.

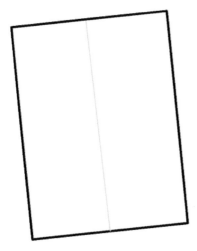

Creativity is allowing yourself to make mistakes. Art is knowing which ones to keep. — Scott Adams

Don't wish it were easier. Wish you were better. — Jim Rohn

The most effective way to do it, is to do it. — Amelia Earhart

Creativity is just connecting things. — Steve Jobs

What we dwell on is what we become. — Oprah Winfrey

With your black pen, practicing your new personal body text font, write six of your favorite quotes on the page, with three on one side, and three on the other. Like this:

Now, using the embellishment ideas in this chapter, make each quote pop.

Once each quote has its own embellishment, ask yourself, "Should any of the quotes be linked together?" If so, add arrows.

If you are having trouble thinking up quotes, you can use these:

If you're not making mistakes, then you're not making decisions. — Catherine Cook

Embellishments are a way to personalize your visual journaling style.

Recap

Embellishments make journaling visual.

You can separate information and make it "pop" on the page!

arrows connect ideas together or create motion on a page.

If you ever use up most of a page, but not all of it, use a horizontal line to create space for a new thought.

Use page borders as a navigation system.

They can be vertical, or horizontal like this one.

Chapter 5

Rediscover your visual vocabulary

There are three different types of simple drawings: pictograms, ideograms, and people figures.

Let's start with the ones we likely learned as children: pictograms.

Pictograms

Pictograms are symbols for a word or phrase.

You may not realize this, but you already have a vocabulary of pictograms in your head.

Exercise: Explore your basic pictogram vocabulary.

Take out a piece of paper that you can recycle later, and your black pen. You can even add some color to this if it feels fun to you.

As quickly as you can, create simple drawings of the following:

- A sun.

- A flower.

- A flame

- A cloud.

- A house.

(Don't turn the page until you do this.)

Chances are, you will end up with drawings that look something like this.

You learned this basic visual vocabulary when you were drawing as a child.

Of course, a circle with lines coming out

of it doesn't look like the real sun, but culturally, we've agreed that is how to draw the sun.

Random sidebar...

The Chinese symbol for the word "sun" is quite different from ours. It looks like this:

ShaoLan Hsueh, creator of *Chineasy*—a clever method of using pictograms to teach Chinese to English speakers—shows the symbol this way.

Hsueh places an English pictogram under the Chinese character to help English-speakers learn Chinese writing more quickly.

Hsueh makes the Chinese character for "sun" look like a window—a pictogram we recognize—then further relies on our pictographic language by using a blue sky and a round yellow sun to make the bridge in our minds between the English pictogram for sun and the Chinese character.

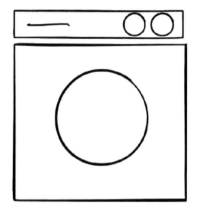

Expanding your pictogram vocabulary

Many of the items we might want to create as simple drawings in a journal aren't part of our childhood pictogram vocabulary.

The thing about simple drawings is that they are simple. So, when creating new pictograms, you just narrow down to the base shapes to communicate an idea of the object.

For example, a washing machine has a simple overall shape.

Once you have the basic shapes drawn, you can add details to further clarify what the object is.

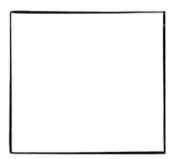

To help identify this square as a washing machine, we can add a few other shapes.

Exercise: build on your pictogram vocabulary.

Pull out a piece of paper you can recycle afterward. Now, with your black pen, draw pictograms of the following items, focusing on simplifying them to their basic shapes.

- Smart phone

- Bicycle

- Coffee

- Computer

How did that feel? This is an exercise you will get better at over time as you practice creating items.

If you are ever completely stumped, search for the object online with the word "icon" after the search term, or check out *The Noun Project* (thenounproject.com) for ideas on how to draw things simply.

Ideograms

Ideograms are symbols for concepts that don't have physical form.

You already have a cultural vocabulary of ideograms.

Exercise: uncover your ideogram vocabulary.

On the same piece of paper you used for the last exercise, find a blank space and quickly draw symbols for:

- Love

- Speech

- Time

- Don't

You probably drew some variation of these:

We know these ideograms because we've seen them before. So, what do you do when you don't have culturally embedded ideogram to illustrate a point in your journal?

You make up your own.

Exercise: Create new ideagrams.

Try coming up with three new ideagrams on your own:

- Brainstorming

- Wishing

- Stuck

- Saving money

Brainstorming may have been the simplest because it is made up of two clear nouns.

You could have drawn a head and a raincloud.

Saving money will have more variants because we have a lot of cultural symbols for money.

You may have drawn a dollar bill, or coins, or the big bags with a $ symbol that robbers stole from banks in old movies.

Did your symbol for wishing include a star? What about pennies in a fountain? Blowing out a candle?

For "stuck" did you include glue, tape or some other adhesive? Maybe you drew a stick figure and a boulder?

Consider that most of our symbols for money are pretty old. That's because our ideogram language was given to us when we were kids.

It takes time to change symbols.

What might a new symbol for money be?

What about "loser?"

What about "okay"?

Why do we underscore our own verbal communication with visuals? Why aren't the words enough on their own?

> **Because we are biologically wired to process things visually.**

We can create new ideograms as we need them by leveraging our existing visual vocabulary or by drawing the simple shapes of existing metaphors. (You are also free to create new ones!)

Gestures are simple motions that visually enhance our verbal communication.

We do something similar on paper when we add simple drawings. (Which most of us enjoyed when we were kids before we developed insecurity over our skill level.)

The drawings in your journal aren't meant to be world-class art.

Why does any of this even matter, anyway?

You may be thinking to yourself....why?

Why wouldn't we just capture words?

Why do the drawings matter?

Consider that you use visuals in your verbal communication—all the time.

Do you know a hand gesture for "he's crazy?"

They simply enhance the way you communicate with yourself.

Which you will discover as you engage the process becomes more and more powerful over time.

Chapter 6

Create symbols for people

Remember this guy?

For most of us, this was our first attempt to draw a human.

Not stellar, but it communicates form. On a page with a bunch of scribbles, this has an identity.

Stick figures

Stick figures are a pictorial vocabulary for

drawing people. I'm not sure exactly when we are taught this, but we are, and it probably evolved out of those first attempts to draw people.

Stick figures are useful because they are

easy to draw, plus, they don't have to be static. We can make the stick figure do things. He can run:

We can also imply gender:

Or practice yoga:

Variations on stick figures

You can do perfectly fine just using stick figures in your journal when you want to communicate a human concept.

The benefit to stick figures is that they are quick and easy to draw, but ask you continue to develop your own unique style of visual journaling, you may want to explore some other rapid ways of drawing the human form.

Fortunately there are some good options that also provide the opportunity to add color.

L people

L people use a capital L for the right leg and a mirrored L for the left under the circle-head. Arms become two quick pen strokes outward.

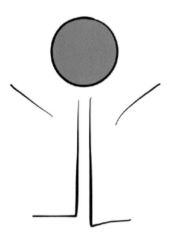

Rectangle people

With a circle for a head and rectangle for a body, arms and legs become quick outward moving lines.

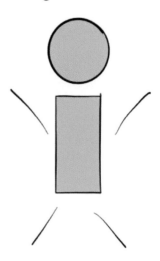

Gingerbread people

Gingerbread people are drawn in the form of the famous cookies. It's like a stick figure, but fatter.

Moon people

Moon people use a "full moon" for the head and crescent moon shapes for arms and legs. Once you get the hang of them, they are super-fast to create.

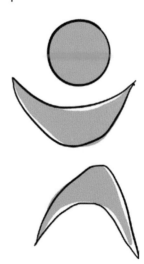

Dot people

Dot people are a spin on the wooden artist mannequins. While they take a bit longer to draw, they are typically more proportionately accurate and can become good practice in eventually drawing more realistic human forms.

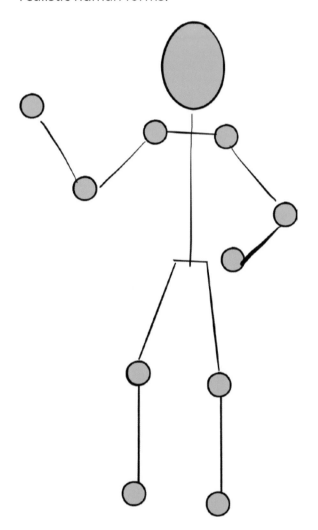

The idea is to choose a method that is enjoyable. And even if you land on one, you can always switch to something else, later. After all, this is your journal.

Faces and expressions

We know from years of inserting emojis into text messages that simple animated forms can communicate expression.

We all know the basic smiley face, sad face and bored face. They are created with five simple pen strokes that we use all the time in our writing:

The parenthesis (

The period .

The line |

The apostrophe '

And the letters **D** and **V**

When drawing quick faces, it's easy to combine these simple pen strokes to make different emotions.

For example, an angry face is simply a V for eyebrows, two period eyes close together and a line for a mouth.

Noses can be created from simple letters, like an **L**, an **O** or a **U**.

A happy face can be made from parentheses for eyebrows, apostrophes for eyes, and the letter D for a mouth.

Worry can be created by using parentheses and periods for the eyes, whatever nose shape you want and an upside down V for the mouth.

Creating expressions using simple shapes is fun—and you don't have to be a cartoonist to get it right in your journal!

The best part about using human forms with expressions is that they are a playful way to communicate something beyond the words that you write in your journal.

They can imply motion and emotion in simple, amusing ways.

For example, in this "Habit Tracker" layout, can you tell how the person journaling felt about their progress?

We can be intimidated by drawing human forms because we've seen so many that are done professionally.

This is your journal.

Do it poorly.

Mess it up!

But keep doing it, because it can be really, really enjoyable.

1. Pictograms are symbols for a word or phrase.

2. Ideograms are symbols for concepts.

3. You can use pictograms and ideograms to illustrate your journal.

4. If you don't know how to draw something, break it down into it's most basic shapes.

5. Find a quick way of drawing people that works for you.

6. Faces can be drawn using simple letter shapes to create expressions.

Chapter 7

Simple layout techniques

Before you start a new journal, there are some layout techniques that can help make it feel more visually organized.

Create an index.

Consider saving the first few pages for an index.

Ryder Carroll—creator of the Bullet Journal method—introduced me to the idea of starting a journal with an index, which has proved to be incredibly useful.

To set up your index, you will want to number all the pages in the journal before you get started. (Some journals—like the Leuchtturm1917 and the official Bullet Journal—come with a preprinted index and page numbers.)

The first three to four pages—depending on how large you write—should be reserved for the index.

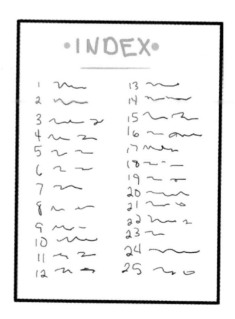

Each time you complete a page in the journal, enter the topic along with a page number so that later, when you want to refer to it again, you can quickly scan the index rather than flipping through pages.

While this takes some time to set up on the front end, it saves tons of time later—especially when referring back to old journals.

complex as adding color-coded lines as page borders for different types of information. (See page 18.)

Your navigation system will be unique to you and will evolve over time.

You don't have to figure it out now. Just keep it in mind for later development.

Determine your personal navigation system.

You can choose to have consistent elements on each page that help you identify the type of information that is on it without having to read the content.

This can be as simple as adding an entry date to the top left of every page, or as

Start each new topic with a headline.

In Chapter 3, we explored headline techniques. Remember that the headline text is usually bigger and bolder than other elements on the page, so it is the first thing you see.

In visual journaling, the headline works the same way it does in magazines. It tells you what information is on the page and where it starts.

Get into the practice of using your personal body text style to capture the bulk of what you are journaling, then using headings and subheadings as navigation elements. This will give you a visual overview of topics when you review your journal later.

Use block quotes and callout boxes to punch ideas.

Magazines format important quotes and information that is related to the article (but not part of it) using block quotes and callout boxes.

This is where the techniques we learned in Chapter 3 come into play.

How to integrate simple drawings into your journaling.

You will find over time that simple drawings become easy to add in your journaling.

But in the beginning, it helps to have a method for incorporating them.

Here are some ideas that are easy to implement:

Use a drawing as part of a text box to create a visual anchor for what you put inside of it:

Use an illustration at the bottom of a quote or block of text:

Add a drawing off to the side of your notes—or really anywhere—to make the information you've written more interesting.

Use an illustration to fill the blank space at the bottom of a list or page:

Exercise: practice adding simple drawings to a journal page.

Pull out a clean sheet of paper. At the top, write "Inspiration" in a headline style.

Under your headline, you can also add a subheading that clarifies what type of inspiration.

Slightly below that, write 3 of your favorite motivational quotes with plenty of space between each in your personal body text font. (Remember we did an exercise similar to this in Chapter 4.)

If you don't have favorite quotes handy, try using the following:

If it's your job to eat a frog, it's best to do it first thing in the morning. – Mark Twain

Drawing is the language of ideas. – Michael Lagocki

Creativity is not a talent. Creativity is a muscle. – Craig Atkinson

Now, to help anchor each quote on the page and enhance the visual interest, add a pictogram or ideogram to each quote.

(If you are using the quotes above, you might be panicking about drawing a frog. No worries. Just draw a sun to illustrate morning.)

There is almost always a simple metaphor to go with an idea. The trick is learning to find it. (Which gets way easier with practice.)

If you happen to be taking notes or writing in your journal, you can also leave space and come back to fill in an illustration later.

1. Save the first few pages of your journal to create an index.

2. Use simple elements to create your own navigation system.

3. Start each new topic with a headline.

4. Use block quotes and callout boxes to punch ideas.

● ● ●

Chapter 8

Different ways to journal

People journal for a lot of different reasons.

The reason you choose to journal will be personal to you. Here are some common journaling methods to help you choose what to include:

Daily Diary

A diary is usually a recap of the day. Often our days can run together, and pausing for a few moments each evening to write about them not only documents memories, but also helps us explore the meaning that we assign to what is happening in our lives.

Idea Notebook

Have you ever noticed that inspiration has a short shelf life?

An idea notebook can be carried around for the purpose of capturing flashes of inspiration as they happen.

It gives you the opportunity to think on paper in real time when an idea strikes. (It is especially useful to keep your journal on your nightstand for those 4:00 am flashes of brilliance.)

The ideas can be unstructured and captured in whatever way makes sense to you:

GTD journal

Many people keep a journal solely to help them ***get things done.***

David Allen (*Getting Things Done,* 2001) revolutionized the productivity genre by coaching people to get things out of their minds and into a system that allows them to spend time acting on things rather than recalling them.

Another highly popular journaling system based on GTD is Ryder Carroll's Bullet Journal. There is a short video on how the system works at bulletjournal.com and searching #bulletjournal or #bujo on Instagram will bring up examples of how others use it.

Gratitude journal

Many successful people have stated that a gratitude practice is the secret to their success.

Creating a dedicated place to consistently write down what we are grateful for can powerfully shift how we are in the world.

Habit tracking

Want to maintain certain habits in your daily life? You can use a journal to log workouts, meditation or prayer time, study, reading, or food/water intake. Writing down progress has been proven effective in helping people reach their goals.

Jen Sincero writes, "If you're serious about changing your life, you'll find a way. If you're not, you'll find an excuse." (*You are a Badass*, 2013)

Emotional journaling

Journaling emotions can be the best therapy we never pay for.

Taking time to write about how we feel allows us to be more present and honest with ourselves.

This can take whatever form we give it, but one way to do emotional journaling is to simply sit down and write out our train of thought first thing in the morning or the last thing before we go to bed. Add visual elements for a powerful—and often beautiful—snapshot of your heart in the moment.

> April 2
>
> Today, I felt overwhelmed by the size of the world. Sometimes I feel so small. and, I wonder if it is possible for me to make a difference.
>
> Politics are loud.
> Suffering is pervasive.
> It's easy to feel helpless in it all.
>
> Then I remember that above all, I have the ability to love.
>
> and that even small love can have big impact.
>
> Today, I plan to practice love.

Minimalist journaling

This is by far the leanest version of journaling. You might want to choose a small journal (5.5 x 3.5 or 4 x 2.4) and keep it by your bedside. At the end of each day, write down the most important thought of the day. Write one thought per page, keeping it to a single sentence, and

illustrating it as you like.

All the white space helps the journal feel simple. And while initially boiling down the whole day into one sentence may not *feel* simple, once we get in the rhythm, it becomes a powerful practice for recording the essence of a day.

Prayer journal

Keeping a prayer journal is a beautiful way to track answered prayers.

One twist on this is "praying in color" a method by Sybil MacBeth. (*Praying in Color*, 2007).

Sybil takes the name of a person she is praying for and draws a shape around it, then embellishes it to hold her attention on the person she is lifting up in prayer. It is a beautiful practice.

which of your values and attitudes are truly you and which parts are cultural (e.g., shaped by the cultures in which you've lived).

Travel journaling

A travel journal is a place to write about the places you've been, experiences you've had, and what they meant to you. Tactically, it is a record of places you've stayed and sights you've seen, but it can also go deeper, exploring how the experience changed you.

Travel journals are popular not only for recording memories, but also for noticing

Vision Boarding

People make vision boards as a creative exercise in picturing what they want their life to be. Think of it like a scrapbook page for "future you."

Whether you have a whole journal dedicated to this or simply a page in a journal you use for something else, there is power in identifying who you most want to become.

Writing words and phrases associated with what you would like to achieve helps bring them into being: not in some magical way, but by focusing your attention. In identifying what you most want for your life and creating a visual representation, you cue your subconscious to make choices aligned with that trajectory.

Having a page or journal dedicated to vision boarding can positively impact your life. (It has definitely impacted mine.)

The Everything Journal

While I've tried maintaining different journals for different things, I never seem to have the one I need when I need it.

My personal journaling practice includes almost everything listed here in a single notebook—even though it means I tend to go through multiple notebooks a year.

By using the layout techniques detailed in Chapter 7, it's easy for me to see what is on each page, and the index helps me find information easily.

The biggest advantage to only keeping one journal is that it creates a single place your mind trusts for everything you want to keep track of—a dependable resource for working with thoughts on paper and referencing them later.

Experiment until you find what works for you.

You may have a couple of false starts when you first start journaling. No worries. Go back to it when you are ready and try something else.

Journaling is a tool. Morph it into whatever you need it to be to make it work for you.

Exercise: Try a method of journaling and commit to it for three months.

Purchase a notebook that will serve as the home for your journaling.

Commit to carrying it with you (along with a black pen and something to add color) for the next three months, and see what happens.

Chapter 9

Journaling exercises to get you started

When you first start journaling, it can be hard to figure out where to start. Here are a few prompts to help you explore different ways to use your journal.

Find an exercise that resonates with you and test drive it.

Exploring emotional memories

Writing about emotions and memories helps us process them. We can spill them out, then look at them objectively to better see context.

Exercise: Write about a time you experienced an emotion or state of being.

Review this list of emotions below and choose the one that pops out at you:

Ambivalent

Angry

Annoyed

Anxious

Awe

Bored

Carefree

Compassion

Courage

Daring

Delighted

Desired

Despair

Disgusted

Elated

Engagement

Envy

Exasperated

Excited

Faith

Fear

Giddy

Grief

Guilty

Handsome/Lovely

Happy

Hopeful

Indignant

Irreverent

Joyful

Love

Melancholy

Panic

Pleasure

Rage

Romantic

Sad

Shame

Suffering

Surprised

Tenderness

Trust

Valued

Wonder

Journal about the very first time you remember experiencing that emotion.

This isn't just about the words. Use the embellishment and simple drawing techniques to fully explore the story.

This type of practice helps us connect events in our lives with how we feel about them. It also helps us process things that happened in our formative years.

Pro tip: Doing this exercise with a close friend and reading each other's entries can be a beautiful way to get to know each other on a deeper level.

— Daring —

The first time I remember feeling daring, I was around seven years old.

There was a field behind my house with a dried up watering hole--which made it perfect for dirt bikes. You could often hear the motors of the bikes and if I stood on the picnic table in my backyard, I could almost see them. They would ride fast down the side into the hole, then catch air as they catapulted up the other side.

One day, my mom let me ride on the back of one of those dirt bikes with my neighbor with the admonition to "hold on tight."

Anecdotal Notes

The idea of anecdotal notes comes from early childhood education.

Teachers capture stories about what happened during the day with their students to get a clear picture over time of the types of experiences the children are having.

Reviewing the notes over time gives them a clearer picture of the themes in their students' lives and how they can help shape the curriculum to enhance learning.

You can do this for yourself.

Each evening, recall your day and capture the scene you remember most. You can do this with words, images, or a

combination of both, to communicate the story.

The event doesn't have to be particularly significant. It only has to stick in your memory. You also don't have to spend a lot of time on this. The more quickly you capture it, the more likely you are to keep this as part of your routine.

When you get to the end of the five days look at your entries. Is there a theme to the stories?

Do you notice anything about each story that helps you realize why your brain held onto it among the other events of the day?

Anecdotal notes are a great way to capture our moments in a world that often moves too quickly for us to process.

As we review them over time, they can help us perceive the richness of our experience and uncover themes in our lives.

Saturday 11.4 —

Today, I stumbled onto a new coffee shop after making a wrong turn off the highway looking for a Starbucks.

Indie coffee shops are hit or miss for me.

But this one had a full walnut colored bar and a well worn path in the stained concrete that led to the counter. The smell of the space revealed they roasted onsite.

There was a wall of books adding to the atmosphere, and as I sat with my cappuccino in the corner, I skipped the wi-fi in order to people watch.

The place was full of regulars who all seemed to know each other.

Those who didn't struck up conversations about the day's upcoming college football games, discussing strategies with each offering an opinion on who would win and why.

As much as I appreciate Starbucks, I deeply enjoyed the coffee shop which had become a place to spend the morning in community before neighbors rushed to meet the day.

It's a wrong turn I'll make on purpose next time.

Mind-map your priorities.

Writing things down on paper can be extremely helpful in revealing the structure of how things fit together.

Exercise: List your priorities and then link all of your activities to them.

Open your journal to a spread of two blank pages. (You are going to need the space.)

Without over-thinking it, list your top five priorities each on a different place on the spread. Leave the right corner blank.

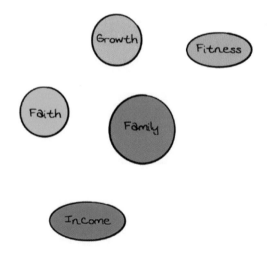

Now, next to each priority, write down all the activities (things you give your time and energy to) that support that priority.

Listen to podcasts
Online course
Daily journaling

Growth

In the lower right corner, write the word, "untethered."

Next to that word, write down all the things you are doing that are not associated with one of your top priorities.

Untethered

Maintain personal blog
Binge watch TV
Serve on HOA
Dance lessons
Online shopping

Looking at your bubbles of priorities and your "untethered" list, are there things you need to cut or say "no" to because they are draining? Are there priorities that are not receiving enough of your time and energy? (Or getting too much time/energy?) What can you realign?

Visually mapping our activities to our priorities can help us step out of "overwhelm" and into a life lived with intention.

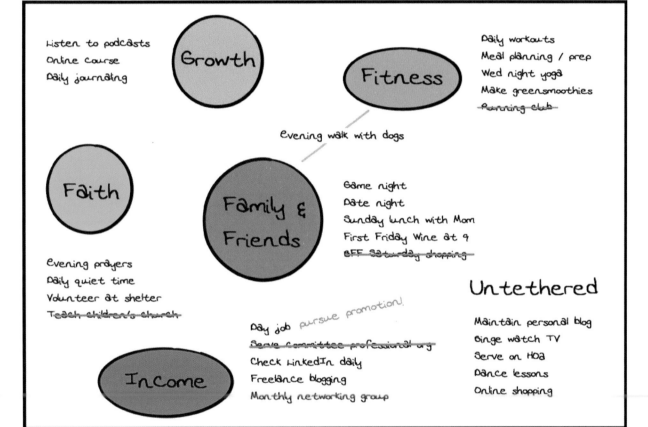

Listen to podcasts
Online course
Daily journaling

Growth

Fitness

Daily workouts
Meal planning / prep
Wed night yoga
Make greensmoothies
~~Running club~~

Evening walk with dogs

Faith

Family & Friends

Game night
Date night
Sunday lunch with Mom
First Friday Wine at 4
~~BFF Saturday shopping~~

Evening prayers
Daily quiet time
Volunteer at shelter
~~Teach children's church~~

Untethered

Day job *pursue promotion!*
~~Serve committee professional org~~
Check LinkedIn daily
Freelance blogging
Monthly networking group

Maintain personal blog
Binge watch TV
Serve on HOA
Dance lessons
Online shopping

Income

Set up a habit tracker.

Have you ever heard the expression: "what gets measured gets managed?"

This can be true in our personal lives.

What habits are you most interested in building? Could visual journaling help you with your follow-through?

When starting a habit, many people set up a layout that covers a month since it takes at least 21 days for new behaviors to become automated, but sometimes that feels overwhelming.

If that's the case for you, it might be easier to focus on smaller increments— like a week.

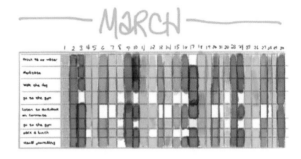

How you track your habits—or for that matter, how many you track—is completely up to you.

Exercise: Pick three habits and track them for a week.

When you decide to track habits, it's best to start small. So what if you started with three habits? Start with three things you want to be consistent with in your life.

Design a layout to track these three habits. If the exercise is effective for you, you may decide to keep it going.

Who knows what changes could happen simply by writing down and tracking what you want to happen?

FeB. 12-18

Goals for this week:
- Spend time outside.
- Workout 5x this week.
- Meditate daily.

Day	Meditate	Workout	Outside
Monday	x	x	x
Tuesday	x		
Wednesday	overslept	x	x
Thursday	x		x
Friday	x	x	x
Saturday	x	x	x
Sunday	x		raining

Try graphic note taking.

Visual note taking engages our brain at a different level than simply listening.

Part of the problem of taking notes in meetings or workshops is that it starts to feel like school. And that can be a problem if you spent hours of every school day feeling trapped in a desk.

A blank page feels different—especially when you add color.

Whether you choose colored pens, pencils, markers or crayons—adding color to your notes makes them more fun to create engaging you more deeply with the topic.

Exercise: Take your journal to your next meeting, workshop, or online course.

There is an art to taking graphic notes in real time—and it will take some practice to become truly good at it.

Often you will wind up capturing the words you want to remember in real-time, then leaving space to go back and add the illustrations later.

Sometimes, the act of illustrating can help you get through the dry or boring parts of a session.

The more you practice, the easier it will be to get the hang of it.

Luckily, even practicing is fun.

How To Make a
TERRARIUM

1. Clean the glass container with soapy water. (You need a glass container that is deep enough for roots.)

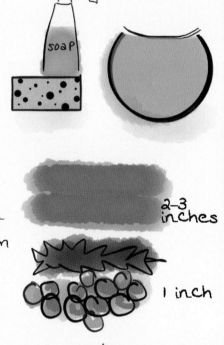

2. Build base. add rocks mixed with charcoal for drainage. Then a layer of moss to keep soil from filtering down. Next put in soil and pack down to remove air.

2-3 inches

1 inch

4. Lightly water your terrarium once a week, or if using cacti, once a month.

3. Choose plants that grow well together. Pick a plant that prefers shade and is tolerant of humidity. Choose plants that will stay small.

Inspire yourself.

We all have dreams and goals that aren't yet part of our current experience, but you can leverage your journal to help you become the type of person who can live those dreams.

Exercise: Pick a quote that inspires you and style the words to make it into art.

Decide which words are the most important and use different header styles to make them "pop." Other words will be written to fill in between the major ones.

Chapter 10

The benefits of visual journaling

There is something about putting black ink and color on paper that is deeply satisfying.

By taking time with this practice, you can expect to experience the following:

- **Clarity.** Thoughts become clearer when plotted to paper and connect more deeply when reviewed.

- **Mindfulness.** The act of journaling makes us more conscious of what we are experiencing.

- **Reaching goals**. Writing down what we want to accomplish is a powerful first step in attaining something.

- **Personal development.** We can increase self-awareness and boost our own emotional intelligence by writing things down. It also creates a record we can review to observe our personal growth.

- **Alleviation of boredom.** Every class, workshop, and meeting becomes more engaging when creating visual notes.

- **Improved self-discipline.** Writing down what we *want* to do, then tracking what we *actually* do, can be a big win in modifying our own behavior to meet a goal.

- **Sparking creativity.** Fleeting ideas can later become real projects when captured. Visual journaling also gives us a way to work with the ideas in a way that reveals their structure.

- **Speed in processing.** Our brains can process entire images that the eye sees for as little as 13 milliseconds; yet processing text takes 225ms when we're reading silently. By adding visuals to your journal, you make the pages easier for your brain to handle.

- **Joy in creation.** Creating something tangible—even something as simple as a journal—gives us a sense of satisfaction. There is a lot of happiness in the process!

60

Appendix

Ideas for pictograms and ideograms

Sometimes the hardest part about drawing something is just getting started.

Here are some ideas for simple graphics to add to your journaling. These can stand for a literal object (pictograms), or they can be used to represent an idea (ideograms). And all can be used to communicate multiple meanings.

You want your drawings for visual journaling to be fast and simple. They don't need to be perfect; in fact, imperfect works best!

Clock, time, waiting, hours, schedule, watch, grandfather, 4:00

Book, read, learn, teach, look up, journal, view, research, plan, dictionary, portfolio

Butterfly, outdoors, hope,
transformation, beauty

Globe, world, environmental, study,
classroom, international

Email, work, write, correspond, memo,
digital communication

Growth, new life, sprout, begin, plant,
plan, germinate, garden

Glass, cup, hydrate, water, (if red, party)

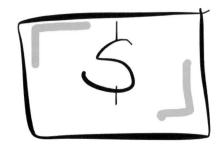

Money, cash, spend, earn, income, salary,
work, shop, buy, taxes, cost

Microphone, announce, speak, share, learn, present, presentation, music, sing, song-writing, amplify

Ship, box, gift, finish a project (ship it!), postage, send, receive, online shopping

Notes, write, scribble, doodle, draw, capture, edit, test, study, list, task

Peach, fruit, healthy eating, grow, groceries, meals, snack, sweet

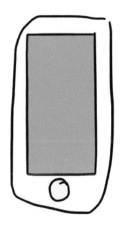

Phone, work, call, talk, email, Internet, connection, distraction

Target, aim, achieve, goals, (if arrow to side: miss)

Sunglasses, beach, summer, cool

Glue, stuck, slow, frustration, make it stick, adhere, cohesion, togetherness

Eyeglasses, smart, brainy

Coffee, cup, aroma, conversation, time with friends, wake up, café, ideas

Ice cream, sweet, childhood, indulgence, treat, savor, yummy, nomnomnom

Passion, love, happiness, internal motivation, finding your why, caring

Wine, winery, friends, Sonoma, celebrate, dine, relax, enjoy

Rocket, forward motion, future, moving upward, taking off, launching

Star, wish, reach, shine, achieve, give,
this is important, remember

Paintbrush, creativity, art, color, create,
paint, do, make, embellish, refinish

Ring, engage, rich, marry, wedding, bling,
aspiration, diamond, shiny

Sun and water, beach, vacation, relax,
peaceful, nature, time off, refresh

How I got into this...

Michael Lagocki scribing for Leadership Network

I first discovered "scribing" when I saw artist, Michael Lagocki, at Leadership Network's *Camp Improv* conference.

My brain was full from all of the amazing speakers I'd heard that day. Speakers like Jim Collins, Mary Crossan, Ron Heifetz,

and others had been sharing nonstop— which meant the information was all running together in my head.

But as I left my seat and filed to the back of the auditorium at the break, I saw the boards Michael was creating. They were notes like I'd never seen before filled with words and images from the sessions. Suddenly, all the big thoughts snapped into place.

I could see how the ideas related to each other and which concepts belonged to which speakers. The clarity was immediate.

That experience hung with me.

I was blown away at the impact the imagery had in helping me process the ideas I'd heard.

Even though I had no idea what I was doing, I started taking crayons with me everywhere, and I began practicing in meetings.

When I started, I was only doing this for myself. It helped my distracted mind pay attention.

As the technique became more and more useful to me professionally, my firm hired Michael to coach me so I could scribe for clients.

Eventually, I served on the board of the arts organization Michael co-founded: ArtLoveMagic. I kept taking my crayons to those meetings, even though I was surrounded by a lot of intimidating talent.

Me scribing for a TEDx Plano event.

I now regularly scribe whiteboard conversations for meetings to help create engagement at a deeper level—which is fun—but, the biggest impact has been in my personal journaling.

Visual journaling is the best way I know to help process ideas. It has impacted my ability to create, think and execute.

The whole reason I wrote this book was so that others could discover this too!

Share how you use this practice on Instagram with the #visjournaling hashtag.

Some thank-yous...

To **Lynn Breeden Black**, who mentioned at a family reunion that of all the things I'd ever written, the article that inspired her the most was the one on visual journaling. It was the moment I decided to create this book.

To **Dara Davulcu**, who gave me the first opportunity to teach this content; and to the professionals at SMPS, whose responsive enthusiasm proved it had value.

To **Robin Eggen**, who introduced me to ink and paper at her kitchen table. (We worked with wild abandon over plum wine and Thai takeout.)

To **Kent Holliday** and the members of the GDA, who affirmed it was okay to bring crayons to a meeting where all the people had impressive titles.

To **Craig Janssen**, who asked, "Do you think you could do this in front of clients?"

To **Danielle Thorp**, I simply love working with you! Thank you for the wit and intelligence you bring to the process.

To **Michael Lagocki and the crew at ArtLoveMagic**, your work continues to create ripples.

And to **John Hutchison**, who never once thought crayons were silly.

About the Author

Cathy Hutchison is an author, public speaker, and joyful wielder of crayons. Her personal mission is to help people find more joy, meaning, and freedom in a world of demands.

Connect with Cathy at visjournaling.com.

You can peek inside her journals on Instagram: @cathy.hutchison.

Printed in Poland
by Amazon Fulfillment
Poland Sp. z o.o., Wrocław

66283374R00047